PLAIN SUGGESTIONS FOR A
REVERENT CELEBRATION OF
THE HOLY COMMUNION

BY THE

REV. CHARLES C. GRAFTON
RECTOR OF CHURCH OF THE ADVENT, BOSTON

WIPF & STOCK · Eugene, Oregon

Wipf and Stock Publishers
199 W 8th Ave, Suite 3
Eugene, OR 97401

Plain Suggestions for a Reverent Celebration of the Holy Communion
By Grafton, Charles C.
ISBN 13: 978-1-60899-359-8
Publication date 2/26/2009
Previously published by Cambridge, 1884

CONTENTS.

——◆——

PLAIN SUGGESTIONS.

I.

The Altar.

THE Book of Common Prayer, in the Institution office, calls the holy table an altar. It should stand at the east end of the church and within the communion rails. This part of the chancel is commonly called the sanctuary.

The reason why the Christian Church came to place its sanctuary, or holy of holies, at the east end of the building probably was to mark the distinction between the Christian and its forerunner, the Jewish Church, which placed its sanctuary at the west end. The Jewish Church, it has been remarked, since it looked forward to the death of Christ, placed its holy of holies toward the setting sun. The Christian Church, built on the triumphant fact that Christ not only died but rose again, and the belief that He will come in glory, symbolizes *her* faith by building her churches towards the rising sun, and placing her altars in the east. As an architectural feature the altar may have a screen of either wood or stone, more or less ornamented, behind it. When from the size of the church the size of the altar is somewhat large, it will be found convenient to have a small space of some eighteen inches in width left between the screen, or reredos, and the altar, in order that persons engaged in the necessary work of cleaning or dusting the reredos, or arranging flowers upon it, may do so more conveniently.

The altar may be of wood or stone. There is no universal tradition in the Church as to the most appropriate material for the altar. While the practice of the Western portion of Christendom has been in favor of stone altars, the Eastern Church has preferred wood, as bringing out more significantly the idea of sacrifice and the offering upon the altar of the cross. For the very practical reason that the priest may be the better heard, as well as the symbolical one of the ascent to Calvary, it is customary to raise the altar on one or more steps. Save in very small churches or chapels, three steps of from four to five inches in height will be found a convenient number. As the priest is obliged, by the directions of the Prayer Book, for the most part to stand while engaged in the altar service, it is important that the altar should be of sufficient height to enable him, in a standing posture, easily to read the altar book.

This matter demands attention, because in portions of the communion service both of the priest's hands are so occupied that he cannot take the book into them; and one cause of the not unfrequent injury done to a clergyman's throat is his being often constrained to read in unnatural positions. Three feet and four to five inches is a good height for an altar. An altar lower than this will compel a priest of average stature to stoop inconveniently. Its length should be in proportion to the width of the sanctuary. The length varies from five feet and a half to twelve feet, in American churches.

Often, but inaccurately, the term "super-altar" is applied to the shelf which runs along the back of the altar, and rests upon it. Properly speaking, a super-altar is a small movable slab of stone, which is placed, as occasion for the celebration of the Holy Communion may require, upon some unconsecrated table or altar. There is no place for such an article among us, unless it be in a sick-room. It is, however, fit and seemly that nothing should be placed on that part of the altar where the consecration takes place save the vessels required for the celebration and the altar book, from which the service is read; for although in pre-Reformation times candlesticks and other ornaments were frequently placed on the altar itself, yet a sense of reverence suggests some change from this mediæval usage. This propriety is secured by the shelf, or retable, as it is sometimes called, placed at the back of the altar, and upon which any needful ornaments may be placed.

The form of this altar shelf resembles that of a box, of the same length as the altar, and from eight to ten inches broad, and from four to six inches high. There may also be shelves or ledges, as part of the reredos, for use in the fuller decorations of the sanctuary customary at Christmas and Easter and other festivals.

It may be observed that, for the most part, our altars are unnecessarily wide. Two feet or two feet and three inches is considered as giving ample width. There is thus scarcely any existing altar upon which a retable may not be placed without any change in the present position of the altar, or trenching upon the space needed in the sanctuary.

Where there is an altar in a church too low and small for convenience and dignity, the fault can often easily be corrected, at little expense, by putting a base of a few inches in height under the altar, and by constructing a plain and simple reredos, which by extending beyond the altar on either side, and also partly inclosing it, will give to the old altar its required dignity. By this arrangement, where as in some places there are special associations connected with any existing altar, the feelings of devout persons will not be pained, as they might be by the removal of an old altar and the substitution of an entirely new one. Reasonable persons will rather be gratified by the care taken of and the beauty given to that which they have so cherished.

The Credence.

In order that the priest may obey the rubric, before the prayer for " Christ's Church Militant," which requires of him, "*Then* to place upon the table as much bread and wine as he shall think sufficient," a small table or shelf, called a credence, is needed upon which the elements can be placed before service, and remain until they are, by the priest, placed upon the altar.

It is a matter of common sense to put the credence where it has anciently been accustomed to stand, on the south side of the sanctuary. There is no mystical reason involved in this. It came about, probably, from the fact that the celebrant at the altar, when about to receive anything brought to

him, naturally turns to the south. This he
does because by so turning he can make use
of his right hand, whereas if he turned to
the north he would be compelled to use his
left.

II.

The Altar Ornaments.

THE altar ordinarily has a covering, called an altar cloth. For convenience, as well as for economy, it is usually divided into two parts. It is thus much easier to remove the altar cloth, when there is need of so doing; and it is more economical, as one portion, the upper one, can be used alone. This portion, which covers the top of the altar and hangs down in front some nine inches to a foot, is called the superfrontal. It may be more or less embroidered, and is commonly finished with a fringe. The other portion, which is oftenest of the same material, is known as the frontal, and falls to the ground covering the west side of the altar.

The Fair Linen Cloth.

The rubric requires that the holy table, at the communion time, shall have upon it a fair white linen cloth. This cloth, in order to fulfill the rubrical directions, should be as wide as the top of the altar. It is not directed to be any wider, but it may be considerably longer than the altar, so as to hang nearly halfway down on either side. As to its ornamentation, it is to be observed that the rubrical direction is not that it shall be "plain," that is, without any ornaments, but that it shall be "fair," that is, in the old English of the rubric, beautiful. The introduction, however, of any color into its decoration seems forbidden by the order that though "fair" it shall be "white." The fair linen cloth may therefore be enriched by having some designs embroidered upon it. Quite a common and simple one is the working of five crosses of the Greek shape upon it; one being placed in the centre, and one in each of the corners. The linen cloth is spread upon the altar as significant that the altar is also the holy table, and the Holy Communion the Supper of the Lord.

The five crosses upon it are symbols of Christ's wounds, and appropriate to the evangelical truth that the sacrifice we feed upon is that of a Lamb that was slain.

The Cross.

Opposition amongst all well-instructed Churchmen to the distinctive symbol of the Christian faith has passed away. The form of the cross can now be seen everywhere in our churches, in the form in which they are built, upon the spires and doors and windows, and adorning the font and chancel. The most fitting place, however, for it is the altar. It is not only our entrance into the Church that is wrought by the power of the cross, but our salvation from the beginning to the end depends upon Christ's grace and the merits of the Passion. This thought Christians should have constantly before them. It is, therefore, most fit that if the symbol of our redemption by Christ's death is to be used anywhere in our churches, it should be placed before us and over the altar, where is celebrated the "sacrament ordained," as the catechism tells us, "for the remembrance of the death of Christ."

Altar Lights.

In many churches, where the chancels are dark, the priest's labors will be greatly relieved and accidents to the sacrament be averted by placing lights upon the altar. The primitive custom is, however, so associated with the original institution, by our blessed Lord, of the Holy Supper deep in the night, when lights were required, that their use has a most commemorative significance.

They are also emblematic of joy; as St. Jerome writes, "In all the churches of the East, when the Gospel is about to be read, lights are kindled, though the sun be shining brightly, not to put the darkness to flight, but to show a sign of rejoicing."

As emblematic of joy they are appropriate to the Holy Communion, and express the truth, that it is a sacrifice "of praise and thanksgiving." Their use is, moreover, so interwoven with the entire history of the holy sacrament, with its primitive celebrations during ages of persecution, with its subsequent long-continued observance at early dawn, with the immemorial practice of all branches of the Church Catholic, Eastern and Western, Greek, Syrian, Coptic, Gothic, Celtic, that we weaken our claim of being primitive, apostolic, and catholic in our usages, if we neglect a custom of the church of God so ancient and so universal. Used, as altar lights are, by the Protestant churches in Germany, Denmark, Norway, and Sweden, their use cannot rightly be said to symbolize any Roman doctrine. Commended by the original Anglican reformers, their use cannot be said to be a revival of mediævalism, or contrary to the spirit of the Reformation, or to symbolize doubtful or erroneous doctrines. Continued in so many Anglican cathedrals, and by the widespread use of so many churches, the practice cannot be said to be contrary to the order of divine worship, as this Church hath received the same. Indeed, so far from tending towards Romanism, or leading on to Rome, their general introduction and

use would do a good deal to show that
our Church is Catholic, though not Papal,
and to remove those prejudices which prevent so many Roman Catholics from join-
ing us. It is, however, of higher impor-
tance to remember that by God's own ap-
pointment lights are the symbol of a sacred
presence (Exodus xi. 4, 24, 25), and are
found in the pattern for our worship re-
vealed to Moses on Mount Sinai, and to S.
John in the Isle of Patmos. (Rev. iv. 5 ;
Heb. viii. 5.) Moreover, the argument is
not without force that as God, after He had
led His people out of Egypt, took Moses up
into the mount, so when God had led the
Christian Church out of Judaism He took
S. John up to heaven, and showed him
the heavenly worship as the general model
and directory, under the free power of the
spirit's guidance, of the worship of the
Christian Church. There, in the ˌmidst of
the Divine Glory, burning on forever in the
eternal noon-day, are the seven golden candlesticks and the seven Lights before the
Throne.

2

III.

The Altar Vessels.

FOR the celebration of the Holy Communion a cup, or chalice, and a paten are
required by the rubrics.[1] The large flagon
sometimes seen in our churches is not mentioned in the Prayer Book. The omission
is not prohibition, unless all omissions are
prohibitions, yet there seems but little need
for it, as a properly constructed chalice will
hold enough to communicate a hundred persons. If there are to be more than this
number at a celebration, there may be two
patens and chalices. Where it is possible, a
priest will prefer to use but one set, as there

---

[1] It is not commonly known that a clergyman may
bring into the country a chalice and paten free of duty.
Articles for the priest's use, which he wears on his person
or carries in his hand, it has been ruled, are free from
import duty.

is something to be said for the feeling that sees in the one chalice and paten a symbol of the truth that we are all partakers of one bread and one cup.

The paten should be made without any base, and so that it may fit into or safely rest upon the top of the chalice. This enables the vessels to be carried together. If the paten has any engraving upon it, it is better to place this on the lower side.

Beside the chalice and paten the following articles will be found convenient for the priest's use in the celebration : —

The Purificator.

A purificator, which is a small square of damask, with a narrow hem, and having a cross marked in the middle. If made of common linen it should be of somewhat coarse quality, as better adapted to absorb water. Its size is determined by the width of the chalice bowl, the diameter of which, being multiplied by three, will give the length of one side of the purificator. The purificator is folded the same way twice, and is so more ready for use. It is used by the priest to

cleanse the sacred vessels at the end of the
service.   The purificators should be kept in
some suitable place in the sacristy.   It is
a more reverent custom to have a fresh and
clean purificator at each celebration than to
use one several times.

The Pall.

Another article of utility is the pall.
It is a piece of cardboard, six to eight
inches square, inclosed in linen.   One side
is marked in the centre with a cross, which
is the common sign placed on all articles
used at the altar.   The size is determined by
the diameter of the paten, which it should
entirely cover.   The pall is used in the celebration to keep the chalice covered, and so
prevent dust, flies, etc., from getting into it,
and to protect it from other defilements.

The pall has a square of linen caught
upon its under side by a stitch at each
corner.   This is so placed as to be easy of
removal in case the linen should by any
chance become stained.   A reverently dis-
posed priest will take some proper measure
to keep the rim of the chalice dry, but if

the lining of the pall should ever become
stained it should be removed and washed
with befitting care, or burnt.

The Chalice Veil.

As it is customary and seemly to cover
the sacred vessels with a napkin or cloth of
some kind, it is well to have one especially
made and set apart for this purpose. This
veil has come to be called the chalice veil.
It must not be confused with the thin lawn
or fair linen one required by the rubric to
cover the elements after the prayer of consecration. As the chalice veil is used for
a different purpose from that of the fair
linen one, its different purpose is signified
by its being made of a different material.
The most serviceable material for the chalice veil is silk, and of a size proportioned to
the height of the sacred vessels. The size
varies from twenty - one to twenty - three
inches square. The veil is made more dura-
ble by being lined with silk, and may have
an inner lining of linen. The sign of the
cross is worked, not upon the centre, where
it would be rubbed and worn, but in the
middle of the lower third of the veil.

The use of the veil is to protect the sacred vessels, while in the vestry, and during the service before the communion, when the vessels are on the credence, from dust, insects, and accidental injury.

There are two other articles which may be mentioned. First "the fair linen cloth," or communion veil, before alluded to, and directed in the rubric, and whose use is peculiar to our own Church. It is not found in the Roman rite, but was required by our reformers, out of reverence for the sacrament. It should therefore not be neglected or laid aside, as is the habit with some advanced ritualists, but rather cherished as a peculiarity of our Church. Symbolically it is said to signify the cloth which after the crucifixion was wound about our blessed Lord's body at His burial. As the Church bids us make it "fair," that is, beautiful, love and reverence will take care to make it as beautiful as it can be made.

The Corporal.

Another article of utility is a square piece of linen called a corporal. It is placed

when in use on the altar for the vessels to
stand upon. It is useful, as will be seen
by subsequent directions, for covering the
paten, during the communion, as the pall is
needed for covering the chalice. It also, by
the manner of its use, protects the chalice
from the danger of being upset; and if
crumbs get upon it, these are more easily
gathered up (as it is movable) than if they
fell upon the larger stationary linen cloth.
The size of it is about sixteen inches square.
It is folded into a smaller square, by being
first folded one way twice, and then folded
twice the opposite way. So folded, it is,
along with the fair linen or communion
veil, kept in a silk case called a burse.

The Burse.

The burse is a case made of two squares
of cardboard covered with silk, and joined
together at the bottom, having the sides
fastened together by a triangular piece of
silk. The burse is open at the top. It
thus forms a pocket or case which can be
opened, within which the corporal and linen
veil may be placed. It is about nine

inches square, and may be adorned on one
side with a cross of the same design as that
on the chalice veil, with which it corre-
sponds in color.

IV.

The Vestments of the Celebrant.

FROM an early date, it has been the custom of the Christian Church, for those set apart to minister in holy things to wear in divine service a distinctive dress. To distinguish the Holy Communion as the only service ordained by Christ himself, an appropriate vestment has ever been worn by the priest officiating at the celebration of it. One fact proves this. There are seven historical churches which have possessed a continuous life since the Nicene era, namely, the Latin, the Orthodox Greek, the Syrian, the Coptic, the Armenian, the Nestorian, and the Georgian. The two former have been parted for nearly a thousand years. The five latter have been parted from each other and from the two former ever since the council of Chalcedon in A. D. 451. Any point on which they are agreed must therefore go back to the middle of the fifth century, and, unless there be some record of its formal introduction, must be part of their consentaneous tradition from a still earlier time. They all do agree in the use of specific eucharistic vestments. There are also written rubrical directions belonging to the third or second century, in one of the oldest extant forms of Christian liturgies (the Apostolic Constitutions), directing the celebrant to put on this vestment. Thus the use of distinctive vestments for the Holy Communion is not, as is sometimes ignorantly supposed, an imitation of Rome, but is a catholic and primitive custom. This eucharistic dress, which was not only recognized but enjoined by the reformers (the rubric regulating its use being still in the English Prayer Book), consists of three principal pieces, namely, an under and an upper garment and a stole.

The under garment is of linen, and is called from its white color an alb. It is like a surplice, only with scantier folds and sleeves, and so better adapted than the surplice to be worn under another garment. Probably the present surplice is only the amplification of the alb, and they are one and the same garment; the alb growing into the present ample Anglican surplice, or shrinking into the Roman form, because used alone. The common sense of the matter is this: that one portion of this clerical dress, called a surplice when used alone, is worn in saying morning and evening prayer, but when the highest act of Christian worship is performed it is but fit that the priest should be *fully* vested, — that is, should wear the upper garment, or chasuble, over his under one, then called an alb. It is to be remembered, however, that this dress cannot fairly be forced into having further doctrinal significance than already belongs to the surplice. The surplice or alb is a vestment, as all the contentions of the English Puritans show, identified with the idea of priesthood, and the chasuble is no more a sacerdotal garb than it. It was the recognition of this fact that led to the Surplice Riots in London some years ago, when the academical black gown was discarded in the pulpit, and the clergy took to preaching in the surplice. If one may use the analogy of an earthly army and its terms, it has seemed to the Church more becoming that the priest should, when he comes to celebrate the one service ordained by Christ himself, be in full uniform.

The alb has for practical purposes a movable collar, which is a small oblong piece of linen which is called an amice. It can be more often washed and changed than the alb, and its object is to protect the stole and chasuble from being soiled about the neck, and is put on in such a way as to fulfill this purpose.

The alb is usually made somewhat long, in order to be usable by all the clergy connected with or visiting a church. It is adjusted to the height of the individual wearing it by a girdle, which also is used to keep the stole in its place. The chasuble, or upper garment of the primitive form, is of a circular or oval shape, having no opening, save one in the centre for the head. The origin of these two parts of the clerical vesture, the alb and chasuble, has been much investigated by German and English writers of late years. Some assert that they are derived from the vestments of the Jewish priests; others that they are derived from the dress of the Roman citizen. The better opinion seems to be that the dress is of Eastern origin, and was the ordinary garb used by the Lord and His Apostles. Their own dress would, of course, be worn by the Apostles into whatever part of the world they went; and would continue to be used, through the conservative spirit of the early Church, as the Church vestments, amidst the various changes of different national costumes. These vestments, having come down to us, help to mark the continuity of our Church with the Church of primitive times. They are part of our rightful inheritance as Christians and Catholics.

They are sanctioned by the usage and order of our reformers. They are by their primitive form and design a constant and visible protest against Romanism and its modern ways. Various symbolical meanings have been invented by wise and unwise minds respecting these vestments. It is as free for any one now as ever to give any spiritual meaning to any one of the garments as may be of help to himself. It is probable that the general style of dress is the same as the one worn by the Lord; it may remind us of Him as the one High Priest.

The material of the chasuble may be of linen or silk, but the latter is preferable. If our Church's order of received worship allows the use of the black silk gown in the pulpit, there is no reason why a white silk one may not be worn in honor of our Lord at the altar.

As the chasuble is the special eucharistic vestment, it should not be worn at any other service.

V.

How to Prepare for the Celebration.

In the vestry, or sacristy, the vessels are prepared in this manner: A simple linen covering is spread upon some suitable shelf or table. Upon this is placed the chalice. A purificator is laid across the top of it. Upon the purificator is then placed the paten, which is nearly flat, and so can rest safely upon it. Upon the paten is placed the pall, and then over all the silk chalice veil is spread. Lastly, the burse, containing within it the corporal and the fair linen veil, is laid on top. In the church, upon the credence, should be placed two cruets, one holding wine, the other water. If there is to be a very large number of communicants, the wine may be in the flagon, but glass is a better and cleaner material than metal for the purpose of holding wine. The kind of bread, whether leavened or unleavened, our Church does not regard a material matter. The kind and form used to have no doctrinal significance. But bread in a wafer form, because always ready for use, and never crumbling, is more convenient for both priest and people. It may also be said to appertain to reverence, as separate from common use. It is, moreover, most probably the same kind of bread used by our Lord at the institution of the Holy Communion, and known as Passover bread now. The altar bread or wafers will be placed on some suitable vessel, which either has a cover, or is covered with some linen cloth. The alms-basin, if there is to be an offering of money, will be placed on the credence, and not on the altar. The altar will have upon it the fair linen cloth, which falls two or more feet at either end, but does not show in front. When the celebrations are very frequent, it is sometimes left upon the altar. It is then protected from dust by a temporary covering of some common stuff, which is removed before the celebration. The altar should have a book-rest upon it.

When the priest is without an assistant, the altar service-book will be placed closed upon the book-rest before the service begins. It is somewhat disputed whether the sacred vessels (not the elements, which are on the credence) should be placed on the altar before the service.

A practical solution of the question is this. If morning prayer is not to precede the communion, let the priest bring in the vessels when he comes in to celebrate. Where the clergyman is alone and morning prayer precedes the communion, he might place the vessels upon the altar before service. In this case he would take the corporal out of the burse and spread the corporal, and then place the sacred vessels, still covered with the chalice veil, upon it.

The priest vests himself in the sacristy, or vestry, the latter and more customary term better denoting the place where the vestments are kept. The vestments needed for the celebration, where there is room for the purpose, may be conveniently laid out for the priest in the following order on some table : —

The chasuble, with the lower half of its two sides turned up, so that, being laid down flat, the exterior is protected from any dust which might be on the table, and the garment is more easily put on by the priest. Upon it are laid the maniple (if used) and stole. The girdle, having been doubled, is placed upon them. Then the alb is laid over them, so folded as to be more readily put on. And lastly the amice is laid on the top. The priest, having washed his hands, then vests himself in the following manner, with amice, alb, girdle, stole, maniple, and chasuble. The cassock, it may be here observed, though now much discarded for the purpose, is as much a home or secular garb as a church one, and can be worn or not, as it is a matter of convenience or comfort. The amice is the first piece put on. It is first placed on the top of the head, the two long strings attached to it hanging down in front. The strings are crossed on the breast and then passed round the body, and brought to the front, where they meet and are tied in a bow-knot. The alb is then put on and next the girdle. The girdle is passed round

the waist and brought to the front, where its
two ends are passed through the loop which
is made by the girdle's having been doubled,
and is so secured. Next the stole is placed
over the neck. The amice is now allowed
to drop down and form a collar covering
the stole and preventing its getting soiled.
The stole, if the celebrant is a bishop, hangs
straight on either side, but if the celebrant
is a priest it is crossed on the breast. It is
kept in its place by the girdle, the lower
portions of which were hanging in front,
and are now brought to either side of the
body. If a maniple is used it is worn on
the left arm; and lastly the chasuble is put
on. As the act of vesting soon becomes a
mechanical one, the priest may profitably
say during the process a few prayers. The
following, or others of one's own selection,
can be used. They can either be learned
by heart or copied out, hung up before the
priest in the place where he is accustomed
to vest.

Prayers while Vesting for the Holy Communion.

At washing the Hands.

Cleanse me, O Lord, from all defilement of heart and body, that I may with clean hands and a pure heart fulfill Thy work.

At putting on the Amice.

Cover, O Lord, my head with the helmet of Thy salvation, that, the assaults of the evil one being repelled, in peace I may offer this service to Thee.

At putting on the Alb.

Cleanse me, O Lord, that, made white, and washed in the Blood of the Lamb, I may serve Thee faithfully, and at last attain to everlasting joy.

At putting on the Girdle.

Gird me, O Lord, with the girdle of Thy love, and extinguish within me the fire of all evil desire, that the grace of temperance and chastity may abide in me.

At putting on the Stole.

Grant me so to bear Thy yoke and minister in Thy name that Thy word may never return to Thee void, but may fulfill that to which Thou sendest it.

At putting on the Maniple.

Grant me so to bear the present burden of labor and sorrow that for love of Thee it may be light, and I may persevere even unto the end.

At putting on the Chasuble.

Clothe me, O Lord, with the robe of Thy righteousness, that trusting only in Thy merits, and resting in Thy love, all that I do may be acceptable to Thee.

(It may be observed that the ancient English use of Sarum directed the priest to say the hymn "Veni Creator" whilst he was robing himself in the sacred vestments.)

Other Prayers that may be Said.

O merciful Lord, incline Thine ear to our prayers, and enlighten our souls by the grace of Thy Holy Spirit, that we may worthily celebrate Thy holy mysteries and love Thee with an everlasting love.

Inflame our hearts, O Lord, we beseech Thee, with the fire of Thy Holy Spirit, that we may serve Thee with chaste bodies, and please Thee with pure souls.

Visit, we pray Thee, O Lord, and cleanse our consciences, that Thy Son our Lord Jesus Christ may, when He cometh, find in us a mansion fitted for His abode.

O God, who in this wonderful sacrament has left unto us a memorial of Thy passion, grant us so to venerate the sacred mysteries of Thy Body and Blood that we may always perceive in ourselves the fruit of Thy Redemption.

VI.

The Order of the Service.

THE following suggestions are for a plain
celebration, where there is but a single
priest. Being vested, and the vessels having been prepared as before described, the
priest takes the chalice by the knob with
his left hand, and, putting the fingers of
his right on the burse, proceeds to the altar.
He ascends to the middle of the altar and
places the sacred vessels a little on one side,
in order to leave room for the spreading of
the corporal. He then takes off the burse
and takes out of it the corporal and veil.
He places the burse on the Gospel side,
standing it up against the retable. He
places the communion veil, still folded, on
the south side, and then unfolds the corporal on the altar and places upon it the
sacred vessels, still covered by the silk veil.

He then goes to the altar book, and opens it. He returns to the centre and goes down the steps, and then turning to the altar says his private prayer; the 43d Psalm is a suitable devotion here, and is frequently used. He says all this standing, upon the general principle given by the House of Bishops in their published resolutions in regard to the posture of the officiating priest. They declared " that as the Holy Communion is of a spiritually sacrificial character the *standing* posture should be observed by him, whenever that of kneeling is not expressly prescribed, to wit, in *all parts* including the ante-communion and the post-communion, except the confession and the prayer immediately preceding the prayer of consecration."

After this short private prayer, the priest ascends to the middle of the altar and goes, according to the rubric, to the " right side." This does not mean to one of the ends of the altar, but to the right or left of the " midst " or middle of the altar. And the phrase " the right side," according to the Sarum Missal, means the Gospel side. The rubric in the marriage service, "standing the man on the right hand," etc., is, however, quoted to show that the "right side" means the Epistle side. The going to the Epistle side at the beginning involves less subsequent change of posture.

The priest then goes to one side, and says there the Lord's prayer and the collect for purity. He then goes to his normal place, which is the middle of the altar, and turning to the people recites the ten commandments. It is well that he should do this without a book; then he goes to the Epistle side, and says there the collect for the day and the Epistle. After the Epistle he comes to the Gospel side, and reads the Gospel. Then he returns to his normal place in the middle of the altar, and recites the Creed, and here he remains, save when going for the elements and communicating the people, throughout the rest of the service.

After the Creed he uncovers the sacred vessels; he takes off the silk veil, and folding it once lays it on the Gospel side. He then places the pall upon it. He takes the paten

and goes to the south, or Epistle, corner of
the altar to receive the bread. If he has
no assistant to bring the elements from the
credence, it would be well to place them
within easy reach. After this the priest returns to the middle of the altar and places
the paten with the breads in it upon the
corporal, in such position that he may turn
over upon the paten the right hand corner
of the corporal. He then takes the chalice,
and, the purificator being on it, he wipes out
the chalice bowl; then he carries the chalice
to the corner of the altar, and takes the
cruet and pours into the chalice a sufficient
quantity of wine, and then, if the universal
practice of the primitive Church is observed,
pours in also a very small quantity of water.
The chalice is then brought and placed on
the corporal, behind the paten, and is covered with the pall. It will be found convenient, for its further use, now to place on top
of the pall, unfolded, the fair linen communion veil.

From this point in the service the priest
will take care that the chalice and paten
when not in use are always covered with

the pall and corporal. The offertory being
made, the priest turns from the right to the
left towards the people, and extending his
hands says, "Let us pray," etc.; and then,
continuing to turn in the same direction, he
completes a circle, and facing again the altar he begins the prayer for the Church Militant. There is no other reason connected
with this movement than that the circle typ-
ifies the whole world, and Christians everywhere. The priest continues the service according to the direction of the Prayer Book.

Here we may note that in saying col-
lects the priest usually keeps his hands together; but in invitations to prayer, and
at the words "Lift up your hearts," and
during the preface, and at the beginning of
the consecration, the hands are separated,
and held facing each other, the elbows resting naturally at the sides. In kneeling
down at the prayer of humble access, it is
well to contract the habit of putting the
hands on the altar under the corporal; by so
doing, the danger of upsetting the chalice is
avoided. On coming to the consecration
the priest uncovers the paten and chalice.

They are uncovered for the consecration and invocation, and then are usually covered during the rest of the prayers.[1]

In communicating the people it is easier for the priest to commence on the south or Epistle side, so that, holding the paten with his left hand, he is more free to distribute from the paten with his right.

Care should be taken to remove any drops which may adhere to the edge of the chalice. After the communion of the people, the chalice is placed in the middle of the corporal. The priest with his finger dries the rim of the chalice, and places his finger to his lips. He places next the paten upon the chalice, and on the paten the pall, and unfolding the communion veil spreads it over the pall.

After the blessing the priest carefully consumes the sacrament remaining. Then, if alone, he goes to the Epistle corner of the

[1] It is the custom of some priests to again uncover the chalice and paten at the words "We beseech Thee accept this our bounden duty and service," etc., when the priest, taking the bread in his right hand, holds it over the chalice, which he holds with his left hand, and raising the two about as high as his breast completes the sentence.

altar, takes the wine cruet, and pours a little wine into the chalice, and, having con-
sumed the wine, a little water and wine is
poured into the chalice over the fingers of
the priest; some water also is poured upon
the paten, which is afterwards emptied into
the chalice, and then the whole is taken by
the priest. The chalice and paten are next
wiped with the purificator, which is left in
the chalice bowl. The chalice is then placed
in the middle of the corporal, the paten
placed upon the chalice, then the pall laid
on the paten, and the whole covered with
the silk veil. The vessels so covered are
moved a little to the south, and the corporal and communion veil are folded. The
burse is then taken from the retable and the
corporal and communion veil are put in it,
and the burse is laid on the top of the silk
chalice veil as it was when it was brought
from the vestry. The priest closes the altar book, and takes the sacred vessels, and
in the same manner in which he brought
them to the altar returns to the vestry.

It will greatly tend to the devotion of the
people and their more frequent attendance

if the priest will study to say the service reverently in manner, quietly and steadily in tone, with moderate rapidity of utterance, with dexterous economy of time at the offertory, without pauses for the introduction of his own private prayers. The service, with a dozen to communicate, can be said with great reverence and devotion, and without any sign of haste, in from twenty-five to thirty minutes. The priest will make after the celebration his thanksgiving to God before leaving the church.

A Prayer of Thanksgiving.

O Lord, Holy Father, Almighty, Everlasting God, who hast vouchsafed not for any merits of mine, but only of Thy great mercy, to feed me a sinner, Thy unworthy servant, with the precious Body and Blood of thy Son our Saviour Jesus Christ, I pray Thee that this Holy Communion may not be for my condemnation, according to my own deservings, but for my pardon and salvation; may it be unto me an armor of faith, a shield of good purpose, a riddance of all vices, an extermination of all evil desires,

an increase of love, patience, humility, and
all virtues, a firm defense against the wiles
of mine enemies, visible and invisible, a
perfect quieting of all my sinful impulses,
fleshly and spiritual, a firm adherence to
Thee, the one true God, and a blessed con-.
summation of my end; and I pray Thee
that Thou wouldst vouchsafe to bring me,
and all those committed unto my care, or
for whom it is my duty and wish to pray,
unto that unspeakable feast, where Thou
with Thy Son and Holy Spirit art to Thy
holy ones true light, fullness of life, everlasting joy, and perfect bliss, through the
same Jesus Christ our Lord.

Another Thanksgiving.

Blessed art Thou, O Lord Jesus Christ,
my Lord and my God. Of Thee, the treas-
ure of my heart, do I lay hold, in whom I
possess all things. From all my necessities
deliver me, O Lord, and make me to be
wholly Thine. Thou art my King and my
Lord; do Thou possess me, and none but
Thee. Thou art my Teacher and my Mas-
ter; teach true understanding and perfect

obedience to Thy law. Thou art my advocate with God the Father; cause that He may turn away His anger from me. Thou art He who shall come to judge the quick and the dead. "Enter not into judgment with Thy servant, O Lord." Thou art my guide and my defender; hold me fast by Thee, and let who will lift up his hand against me. Thou wast made a victim for me; my trust hath been in Thee, O Lord, therefore shall I not fall. Thou art my Saviour and Redeemer; finish Thy work, and let not Thy labor be of none effect. Thou art the portion of my inheritance, my portion in the land of the living. Do thou restore my heritage unto me. Thou art my glory, my crown, and my exceeding great reward; admit Thou me to those good things which Thou hast prepared for them that love Thee. O Jesus, pour into me Thy grace, wisdom, love, humility, that I may be able perfectly to love Thee, to praise Thee, to serve Thee, and to glorify Thee, now and evermore. — *Amen.*